COOL PETS for Kids

Reptiles and Amphibians

DAWN TITMUS

PowerKiDS press.

Published in 2019 by The Rosen
Publishing Group, Inc.
29 East 21st Street, New York, NY 10010

Cataloging-in-Publication Data

Names: Titmus, Dawn.
Title: Reptiles and amphibians / Dawn Titmus.
Description: New York : PowerKids Press, 2019. | Series: Cool pets for kids | Includes glossary and index.
Identifiers: LCCN ISBN 9781538338100 (pbk.) | ISBN 9781538338094 (library bound) |
ISBN 9781538338117 (6 pack)
Subjects: LCSH: Reptiles as pets--Juvenile literature. | Amphibians as pets--Juvenile literature.
Classification: LCC SF459.R4 T58 2019 | DDC 639.3'9--dc23

Text and editor: Dawn Titmus
Editorial Director: Lindsey Lowe
Children's Publisher: Anne O'Daly
Design Manager: Keith Davis
Picture Manager: Sophie Mortimer

Photo acknowledgements:
t=top, c=center, b=bottom, l=left, r=right
Alamy: Cattie Coyle 10-11, Design Pics Inc 26-27, Juniors Bildarchiv GmbH 7b, Milton Solomon 17b, Nature Picture Library 27b, Top-Pets-Pics 7t; Dreamstime: 9bl, Cathy Keifer 11t; iStock: Grafner 15, kali9 12t, Mark Kostich 13b, ross1248 22, sdominck 17t, SerrNovik 4t, Sirikornt 13t, Suwat Siriutcharungc 25t, Snowleopard1 27t, the4js 14-15; NaturePL: Premaphotos 12b; Shutterstock: Alikosina 7c, Blur Life 1975 8r, 23t, Vince Bradley 19b, Brownyn Photo 21t, BW Folsom 8rb, Pei Chung Davy 29t, Marta Cobos 8lb, cynoclub 6, Dobermaraner 20, Lukas Gojda 4-5, Tawat Hantrakool 4br, Eric Isselee 1c, 24, Maria Jeffs 1r, Matt Jeppson 29c, D. Kucharski/L. Kucharska 25b, Luis Louro 3, Mehdi Photos 9t, Nick Norman 9br, obkung 16, Olhastock 4bl, paytai 21b, Dmitry Petlin 18, picturepartners 7c, Ondrej Prosicky 14, reptiles4all 5, Swapan Photography 8lt, Camilo Torres 23b, Tremor Photography 29b, Tsekhmister 1l, Marek Velechovsky 11b, werg 10, Melani Wright 19t, xpixel 8rt.

Manufactured in the United States of America

CPSIA Compliance Information: Batch #CS18PK: For Further Information contact Rosen Publishing, New York, New York at 1-800-237-9932.

Contents

Which Reptile or Amphibian?

Reptiles and amphibians are fascinating to watch. However, they do need care and attention, so make sure you are well prepared before you take one home.

Life Spans

Many reptiles and amphibians have long lives. Some frogs can live for up to 15 years, snakes up to 20 years or more, and pet turtles for 50 years or more. Make sure you are prepared to look after your pet for as long as it lives!

Rescue a Pet

Rescue centers and shelters are full of pets that need new homes. Think about giving a pet from a rescue center a forever home. Rescue centers can also give advice about the best way to care for your new pet.

Buying a Pet

If you cannot find a pet at your local rescue center, buy one directly from a breeder or a good pet store. Check out notices for pets at the vet. Make sure you buy a healthy pet. Look for clear, bright eyes, and no discharge from the eyes, nose, or mouth.

Local Laws

Be sure to check your local laws. In some states, it's illegal to keep certain reptiles and amphibians as pets.

The Right Pet for You?

- ✔ Can you provide a safe home for your pet?
- ✔ Do you have the space for a tank for your pet?
- ✔ Do you have the time to care for your pet every day over many years?
- ✔ Can your family afford the costs to buy the tank and food and pay vet bills?

Read On ...

Reptiles and amphibians are awesome pets. They are less demanding than some pets, but it is important to choose the right one for you. This book tells you about six of the most popular types and shows you how to make a fun snake toy. You will also find some fascinating facts about your new friends!

What You Will Need

You will need special equipment to make your pet as safe and comfortable as possible, including heating and lighting.

What You Need

- ✔ Tank large enough for your pet.
- ✔ Daylight lamp and heat bulb or heat mat.
- ✔ Lining material for the tank and hiding places.
- ✔ Food and water containers.
- ✔ Humidity gauge and thermometer.
- ✔ Small-animal keeper (for live food).
- ✔ Filter system, water heater, and water conditioner for aquatic turtles.

Setting Up the Tank

You will need a glass or plastic tank large enough for your pet. Reptiles and amphibians are cold-blooded—they need outside sources of heat to warm their bodies. Usually, you will need to heat the tank and keep the humidity at the right level. Use a thermometer to check the temperature and a gauge to check the humidity.

Aquatic Pets

Aquatic turtles need water for swimming. Keep the water clean with a filter system and water conditioner. You will also need to use a water heater to keep the water at the correct temperature for your pet. Change the water about once a week to keep your pet healthy.

Live Food

Some pets such as lizards eat live food, including mealworms and crickets. If you keep the live food at home, you will need a secure enclosure for it. You will also need to give it food and water.

Lighting

Many captive reptiles and amphibians need special lighting over the tank to mimic daylight. This keeps them healthy. The daylight lamps should be left on for 10 to 12 hours a day.

Housing Your Pet

Your pet's housing should be as much like its natural habitat as possible. Find out where it lives in the wild to help you set up its home.

Lining the Tank

Line the bottom of the tank with substrate, such as bark, moss, sand, or coconut fiber. Find out what type of material is best for your pet. Some pets like to burrow, so they will need a deep layer of substrate.

Coconut fiber

Sand

Bark

Moss

Inside the Tank

Make sure your pet has somewhere to hide in the tank. Pets can get stressed if they do not have places to shelter. Artificial plants or bark help make your pet's home more natural.

Water Turtles

The tank for aquatic turtles should be big enough to hold 10 gallons (38 liters) of water for every inch (2.5 cm) of the turtle's length. Turtles need a warm, dry surface for basking and a ramp for climbing onto it. Use a light to heat the basking zone to the correct temperature for your pet. Put a cover on the tank to protect your turtle from other family pets.

Special Lighting

Many reptiles and amphibians need 10 to 12 hours of daylight a day to stay healthy. Do not put their tank in direct sun. Instead, use special lighting over the tank that has ultraviolet A (UVA) and ultraviolet B (UVB) rays to mimic sunlight.

Humidity Levels

Some reptiles and amphibians live in deserts in the wild and need a low level of humidity in the tank. Others need more humid conditions. Find out what humidity your pet prefers. Use a water sprayer to mist your pet's tank if it is too dry.

Feeding Time

Different types of reptiles and amphibians need different types of food. Find out what food is best for your pet and how often you need to feed it.

Prepared Foods

You can buy food made specially for your type of pet at the store. Bearded dragons, for example, need insects, vegetables, and fruit in their diet. You can buy pellets that contain everything they need to eat. Pet stores also sell pellets for turtles and iguanas.

Water

Provide fresh water for your pet every day. Amphibians absorb water through their skin. Do not give your pet water straight from the faucet as it contains chemicals that can harm it. Use bottled spring water or water that has been treated to remove the chemicals and change it every day.

Insect Foods

Lizards, frogs, and salamanders eat a variety of insects. Many lizards like live food, such as crickets. Some lizards eat only plants. Some frogs eat locusts, cockroaches, and pinky mice. You may need to give your pet extra minerals and vitamin D. You can buy vitamin and mineral powder at the pet store.

Snake Food

In the wild, snakes eat mammals, birds, amphibians, fish, and other reptiles. Feed a mouse to your adult pet snake every 7 to 10 days. You can buy frozen mice from pet stores or online. Make sure the mouse is thawed to room temperature first. Do not feed your pet snake live food. It may bite or injure your pet.

Staying Healthy

Providing your pet with a comfortable home, fresh water, and the right kind of food will help keep it healthy. Check your reptile or amphibian every day for signs of sickness.

Fungus

Aquatic turtles can get fungus growing on their legs and in cracks in the shell. Amphibians can get fungal diseases, too. Look for a white, cotton-like substance. It can be caused by dirty water or the tank being too humid. If your pet has fungus, take it to the vet.

Mites and Ticks

Mites and ticks can cause skin problems and spread diseases. Snake mites are usually black and are often found around the eyes. Lizard mites are red to orange. They hide in folds of skin or between the toes. Ticks are larger than mites. Take your pet to the vet if you see mites or ticks.

Good Hygiene

Amphibians have delicate skin. Don't handle them unless you have to. If you handle your reptile, wash your hands well afterward. Reptiles and amphibians carry bacteria, which can cause disease in humans. Clean the tank every two to three weeks and wear gloves when cleaning.

Signs of Sickness

- ✔ Your pet is not eating or drinking.
- ✔ It has swollen joints.
- ✔ It is hiding most of the time.
- ✔ It has runny eyes, nose, or mouth.
- ✔ Its droppings are runny for more than two days.
- ✔ It has lost weight.
- ✔ Its skin is discolored.

Take your pet to the vet if you think it may be sick.

Shedding Skin

Reptiles and amphibians shed their skin several times a year throughout their lives. Problems can occur with shedding if the tank is too dry. Spray it lightly with water to help your pet loosen the skin. Once your pet has finished shedding, remove the dead skin from the tank.

In the Wild

Reptiles and amphibians live all over the world, except for polar regions. Reptiles include lizards, turtles, snakes, crocodiles, and alligators. Amphibians, such as frogs and toads, are animals that can live both on land and in water.

Lizards

Lizards live in most parts of the world, including the Americas from southern Canada to the southern tip of South America, Europe, most of Asia, Africa, and Australia. They usually live in warm climates, but some have adapted to live in cooler regions.

Amphibians

Usually, amphibians are animals that spend part of their life in water and part on land. Most young amphibians live in water and have gills to breathe, and the adults live on land. But some amphibians live entirely on land, and others spend their whole lives in water. Frogs, toads, caecilians, and salamanders are all amphibians.

Snakes

There are more than 3,200 different species of snake. They live all over the world except for polar regions, Iceland, Ireland, and New Zealand. Sea snakes live in all the oceans apart from the Atlantic Ocean. Snakes are more numerous in warm places. Most snake species lay eggs, but those that live in cold places generally give birth to live young.

Turtles and Tortoises

Tortoises live entirely on land. Aquatic turtles live in freshwater. Sea turtles live in the oceans, and terrapins live both on land and in water. There are more than 300 species of turtles and tortoises. They have four legs and a hard, protective shell made from bony plates. They live in deserts, tropical forests, and lakes on all the continents except Antarctica, and in seas all over the world.

Red-eared Slider

The red-eared slider is one of the most popular pet turtles. It is a good pet for beginners, but it needs a spacious tank.

Where in the World?

The red-eared slider comes from the eastern United States and northern Mexico. It has been introduced to many areas of the world. It lives in slow-moving freshwater creeks, as well as in lakes and swamps. It is illegal in the United States to sell a turtle that has a shell less than 4 inches (10 cm) long.

The red-eared slider has red ear patches on its head.

Breed Profile

Red-eared sliders are semiaquatic turtles. They spend some time in water and other times basking on land in the wild. Their skin is green with yellow stripes. Adult red-eared sliders grow to about 12 inches (30 cm) long. Females are slightly larger than males. Red-eared sliders can live for more than 20 years.

Looking After Me

Feed turtle pellets to your pet every other day. You can also give it dark, leafy greens, freeze-dried shrimp, and crickets. Feed your pet in a separate container so it does not make a mess in its tank.

- ✔ Keep the water temperature at 75 to 85 °F (24 to 29 °C).
- ✔ Use a lamp to heat the basking area to 85 to 90 °F (29 to 32 °C). Also use a daylight lamp.

Corn Snake

The corn snake is a good family pet. They are easy to handle and are among the most popular pet snakes.

Corn snakes can become quite tame.

Where in the World?

In the wild, the corn snake lives in the eastern United States, north to New Jersey and west into Utah and Colorado. It is often found in cornfields and corn supplies, which is how it got its name.

Breed Profile

The corn snake is orange to red-brown and comes in a range of patterns. In the wild, they live mostly on the ground, but they also like to climb. Adults grow to 4 to 6 feet (1.2 to 1.8 m) long. Pet corn snakes can live from 12 to 20 years.

Looking After Me

The corn snake needs a tank that is at least 20 gallons (78 liters) with an escape-proof lid. Provide hide boxes, such as PVC pipe or a hollow log, and branches for climbing.

- ✔ Feed your pet freshly killed or frozen and thawed rodents every 7 to 10 days.
- ✔ Use a heat pad or light to create a warm zone of 85 °F (29 °C). The cool zone should be in the low 70s °F (20s °C).

Leopard Gecko

Leopard geckos are curious lizards that are usually easy to handle. They make excellent pets for the beginner reptile keeper.

The leopard gecko is a small lizard with large eyes and a long tail.

Where in the World?

The leopard gecko comes from Afghanistan, Iraq, Iran, northwest India, and Pakistan in South Asia. In the wild, it lives in dry and semidry desert regions and grasslands.

Breed Profile

The leopard gecko gets its name from its yellow skin covered with brown stripes or spots, which looks like leopard skin. Adults grow 8 to 10 inches (20 to 25 cm) in length. Males are larger than females. Leopard geckos are nocturnal and are rarely seen during the day. They can live for 8 to 10 years, but sometimes live as long as 20 years.

Looking After Me

House your pet in a 10- or 20-gallon (38 or 78 liter) tank and provide it with hide boxes.

- ✔ Feed your pet live food such as crickets every other day. Dust the food with vitamin and mineral powder every other feed.
- ✔ Heat a basking zone to 87 to 90 °F (30 to 32 °C). The cool zone can be 74–80 °F (23–27 °C).

Bearded Dragon

The bearded dragon gets its name from its ability to expand its spiny throat pouch, or "beard," when it is alarmed.

Where in the World?

The bearded dragon comes from central and eastern Australia. It lives in deserts, dry forests, and scrublands.

The "beard" is a throat pouch.

Breed Profile

The bearded dragon has a triangular head and spiny scales on its body. Its color can be brown, tan, gray, green, orange, or red. Adults can grow up to 2 feet (60 cm) long, including the tail. Bearded dragons can become quite tame and will feed from their keeper's hand. They usually live for 7 to 10 years.

Looking After Me

House your pet in a tank with hide boxes, logs for it to climb on, and a dish of water large enough for it to bathe in.

- ✔ Heat the basking zone to 95 to 110 °F (35° to 43 °C). Also use a daylight lamp.
- ✔ Feed your pet live food, such as crickets, four or five times a week. Also feed it chopped vegetables and fruit. Dust the food with calcium and vitamin powder once a week.

Pacman Frog

The Pacman frog is easy to care for and is a good pet for the beginner amphibian keeper. Take care—they don't like to be handled!

The Pacman frog gets its name from the Pac-Man computer game. The character Pac-Man has a large mouth!

Where in the World?

The Pacman frog lives in Argentina, Uruguay, and southern Brazil in South America. It lives near freshwater marshes and pools in forests. It is also called the Argentine or ornate horned frog.

Breed Profile

The Pacman frog has a large mouth and hornlike upper lids above its eyes. It comes in a range of colors, including yellow, green, orange, and brown. Females grow to 4 to 6 inches (10 to 15 cm) long. Males are smaller. They are usually almost as wide as their length. Pacman frogs can live up to 10 years.

Looking After Me

House your pet in a 10-gallon (38 liter) tank lined with damp material such as coconut fiber. Give it fresh, clean water every day.

- ✔ Heat the tank to 75 to 82 °F (24 to 28 °C).
- ✔ Feed your adult pet about once a week. It eats earthworms, locusts, cockroaches, crickets, and mice. Do not handle your pet—it may bite!

Tiger Salamander

Named for the tigerlike pattern on its body, the tiger salamander is a cute pet. It can learn to recognize its keeper and "beg" for food!

The tiger salamander has attractive stripy markings.

Where in the World?

There are several closely related species of tiger salamanders. They are found throughout the United States, as well as in southern Canada and northern Mexico. In some states, it is illegal to own a tiger salamander. Check the laws in your state before you buy this pet.

Breed Profile

Tiger salamanders can be olive green, black, or yellow with brown, black, yellow, or gray markings. They have a rounded snout with an upturned mouth that makes them look like they are smiling! They grow up to 6 to 13 inches (15 to 33 cm) long. They can live for between 15 and 20 years.

Looking After Me

Tiger salamanders like to burrow. Line the tank with a deep layer of substrate such as coconut fiber. Keep the substrate damp in half the tank.

- ✔ Feed your pet live crickets, earthworms, and cockroaches two to three times a week.
- ✔ There is no need to use special lighting or to heat the tank. A temperature of about 70 °F (21 °C) or lower is fine for your pet.

Make It!

Snake Toy

Make a cute snake from some egg cartons and paint it any color you like. Pull it along to make it slither across the floor.

You Will Need:

- Cardboard egg carton
- Scissors
- Tempera paint in two or more colors
- Paintbrush
- Wool or string
- Red construction paper
- Glue
- Googly eyes

1 Cut out six cups from the egg carton. Cut off any ragged tops.

2 Paint the cups in two or more different colors inside and out. Or you could paint the cups in one color and add stripes or spots in another color. Let the paint dry.

3 Arrange the cups in a line. Stand the head on its side so the open side faces forward.

4 Ask an adult to make small holes on either side of the five body cups. Make one hole in the head cup.

5 Push a long piece of string or wool through the holes to tie the cups together. Tie a knot inside the head. Leave a length of wool or string so you can pull your snake along.

6 Cut a forked tongue shape from the construction paper and glue it to the inside of the head. Glue two googly eyes on top of the head.

Did You Know?

Most snakes have brown or black coloring that blends in with their surroundings. However, some snakes are brightly colored. The bright colors of the coral snake warn predators not to attack.

The largest turtle in the world is the leatherback sea turtle. It can grow up to 8 feet (2.4 m) in length.

Mexican beaded lizards and Gila monsters are lizards that kill their prey using poison in their saliva.

There are more than 10,000 reptile species and more than 7,700 amphibian species.

Some frogs, such as the female Surinam toad, carry their eggs on their back until they hatch. The male midwife toad carries the eggs glued to his legs.

The tuatara is a type of reptile found only on small islands off the coast of New Zealand. They can live for 100 years or more.

The Aldabra giant tortoise can live for 150 years or more. A male called Jonathan is thought to be the oldest living tortoise in the world. It is thought he hatched in 1832.

The fire salamander has large poison glands on its body. It can squirt poison at prey from glands on its back.

Glossary

burrow make a tunnel or hole in the ground by digging.

fungus (plural, fungi) type of simple life-form, such as mold. Some fungi can cause disease.

gland organ in the body that produces a substance, such as sweat.

habitat place an animal or plant naturally lives.

humidity amount of moisture in the air.

iguana large lizard that lives in Central and South America.

mealworm young form of a beetle, often used as pet food.

mimic create the effect of something.

mineral substance found in food that is important for good health.

mite very small animal that lives on plants, animals, and food.

pellet small hard ball of food for animals.

pinky mouse young mouse without fur.

predator animal that kills other animals for food.

saliva liquid produced in the mouth.

scrubland area with small bushes and trees.

substrate layer of material that lines the bottom of a tank.

tick very small insect that attaches itself to a larger animal and feeds on it.

ultraviolet (UV) describes light rays found in sunlight that cannot be seen.

vitamin D natural substance that is important for healthy bones, found in some foods and created by exposure to sunlight.

water conditioner substance used to remove harmful chemicals from water.

Further Resources

Books

Hamilton, Lynn and Katie Gillespie.
Turtle (Caring for My Pet). AV2 by Weigl, 2016.

Lowenstein Niven, Felicia
Learning to Care for Reptiles and Amphibians (Beginning Pet Care with American Humane), Enslow Publishers, 2010.

Wilsdon, Christina.
Ultimate Reptileopedia: The Most Complete Reptile Reference Ever. National Geographic Kids, 2015.

Websites

Due to the changing nature of Internet links, PowerKids Press has developed an online list of websites related to the subject of this book. This site is updated regularly. Please use this link to access the list:

www.powerkidslinks.com/cpfk/reptiles

Index